Brai

Great Color
Optical
Illusions

Keith Kay

Sterling Publishing Co., Inc.

New York

Library of Congress Cataloging-in-Publication Data

Kay, Keith
   Great color optical illusions / Keith Kay.
     p. cm.
   ISBN 0-8069-8813-4
   1. Optical illusions in art. 2. Visual perception. I. Title.

   N7430.5 .K38 2002
   701'.15–dc21   2001055147

10 9 8 7 6 5 4 3 2

Published by Sterling Publishing Co., Inc.
387 Park Avenue South, New York, N.Y. 10016

Distributed in Canada by Sterling Publishing
c/o Canadian Manda Group, One Atlantic Avenue,
Suite 105, Toronto, Ontario, Canada M6K 3E7

Distributed in Great Britain and Europe by Chris Lloyd
at Orca Book Services, Stanley House, Fleets Lane,
Poole BH15 3AJ, England

Distributed in Australia by Capricorn Link (Australia) Pty. Ltd.
P.O. Box 704, Windsor, NSW 2756 Australia

Printed in China

Sterling ISBN 0-8069-8813-4

Optical illusions come in all shapes and sizes. They provide us with the curious pleasure of demonstrating how blind we are to what we see.

I hope you will enjoy this colorful collection of optical illusions. It will keep you puzzled, amused, and entertained by proving that seeing is sometimes deceiving.

Sherlock Holmes is reading a
headline. What does it say?
Are you sure?

Is the zebra black with white stripes or
is it white with black stripes?

The name of this old-time print is "Time Passes." Why do you think it was given this title?

Can you figure out why this picture is titled "Before and After Marriage"?

This picture shows a young girl and her grandmother. Can you find both of them?

This is a real postage stamp of Daniel Webster. If you turn it upside down and look very carefully, you will see someone else. Who do you see?

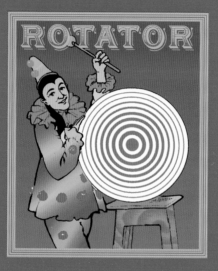

Slowly rotate this page in a circular
motion. What happens to the clown's
drum? What's unusual about the
word "rotator"?

Stare at the red dot for about 30 seconds. Try not to blink. Then look at a blank wall or a sheet of white paper. You will see a famous lady. Who is she?

MADAM I'M ADAM

Do you notice anything unusual about this eaten apple? The clue is in the phrase. What's unusual about the phrase?

This attractive landscape print holds a secret. Can you find the landlord?

Place a pencil along the line of the
two arrows. What happens to the
color of the circle?

How can you get the bee to move
closer to the flower?

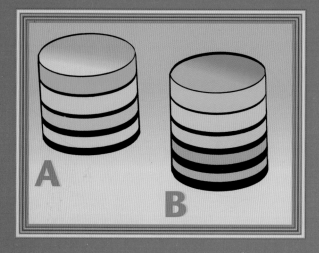

Which pile of disks has the same
height and width?

What is this a picture of?

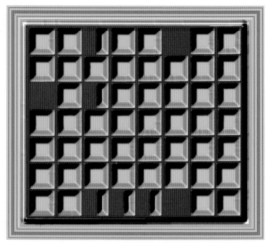

Can you discover the secret word that has been concealed in this design?

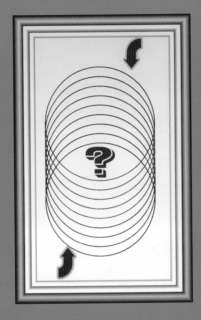

You can look through this coil
from either end. Keep staring at it
and what happens?

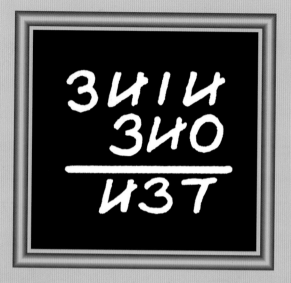

This mathematical problem is wrong.
How can you correct it?

What do you see in this
strange picture?

Can you find this baby's mother?

The soldier is pointing his finger straight at you. Move your head from left to right. What appears to happen?

Otto is holding a cake. One slice is missing. Can you find it? There is also something odd about the name "Otto." What is it?

Does this sign say "knowledge" or
does it say "ignorance"?

How can you get the boy to take a
spoonful of his medicine?

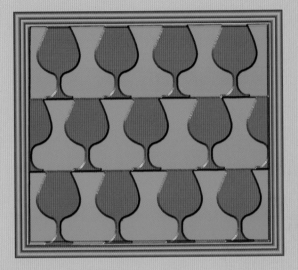

What do you see, purple glasses
or green vases?

Will the girl ever get to the bottom step on this flight of stairs?

Are these two painted stripes exactly the same size, or is one bigger than the other?

What bird do you see here,
a hawk or a goose?

Can you figure out what
these shapes represent?

BACCHUS

This is a picture of the Roman god Bacchus. If you look very carefully you will also see a picture of Romeo and Juliet. Can you find them?

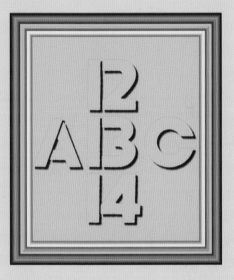

What do you see in the middle of the frame? Is it the letter B or the number 13?

The brown shapes may seem unrelated, but they form a figure. It is an example of a "closure." Can you see what the figure is?

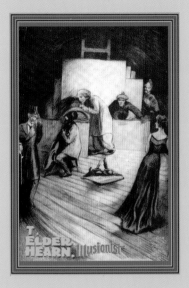

This is a poster of vaudeville
performer, T. Elder Hearn. He was a
quick-change artist. What do you see
in this publicity print?

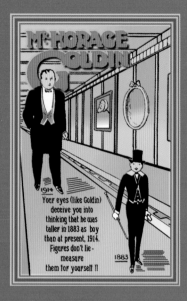

Magician Horace Goldin used this flyer to advertise his theater shows. Who looks taller, Goldin as a man or as a boy?

Stare at the yellow dot for about
30 seconds. Try not to blink. Now
stare at a piece of white paper.
What do you see?

How many cubes can you see,
seven or eight?

Clowns work in the circus. Here's the clown. Where's the circus?

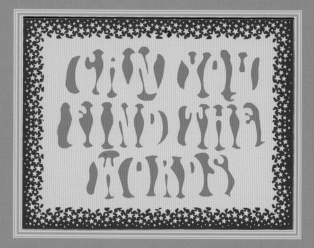

Can you find the hidden message?
What does it say?

The hooded monk has a bizarre
secret. What is it?

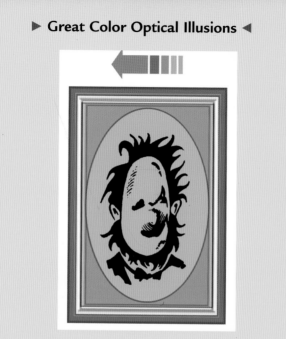

Can you figure out what this Victorian puzzle shows? Is it an animal, vegetable, or mineral? Try looking at it from different angles.

Only one of these sets of letters says
something when viewed in a mirror.
Can you figure out which one it is
before using the mirror?

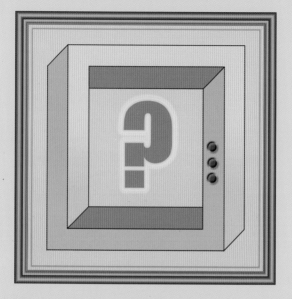

Are the three dots on the inside or the outside of this frame?

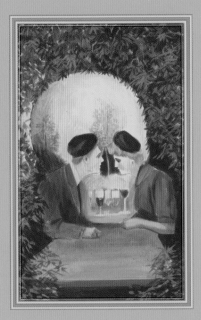

This picture is based on what were known in Victorian times as "Fantasy Faces." What do you see?

Is there life after death?

At first glance, we see a pig.
But where is the farmer?

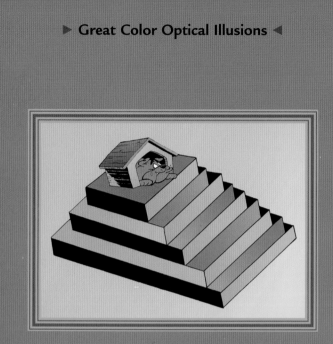

Do you notice anything unusual
about this flight of steps?

Can you see where Napoleon
is hiding?

What do you see in this picture:
Blue arrows or yellow arrows?

Can you spot the farmer
in this landscape?

The shop was selling poor-quality dice at 50¢ each. This was not the correct price. Can you figure out what was the real price?

What playing card is represented in this illustration?

The sailor is looking through his telescope to find his girlfriend. Can you find her?

This old sketch is called
"Under the Mistletoe."
What's odd about this drawing?

What's so special about
this set of numbers?

What happens when you rotate this page in a circular motion?

What is unusual about
this sentence?

This soldier is looking for his horse.
Do you have any idea where it is?

Can you discover why this old British
colonial patriotic design is called
"The Glory of a Lion Is His Mane"?

This is the island of St. Helena.
Where is Napoleon?

Read the words in the hat very slowly.
What do they say?

??? FINISHED FILES ARE THE RES-ULTS OF YEARS OF SCIENT-IFIC STUDY COMBINED WITH THE EXPERIENCE OF YEARS.

Using only your eyes, count the number of F's in the above sentence. How many are there?

What do you see in this picture?

Napoleon's supporters used to wear violets as a sign of their allegiance. This print hides the faces of Napoleon, Maria Louisa, and the young king of Rome. Can you find them?

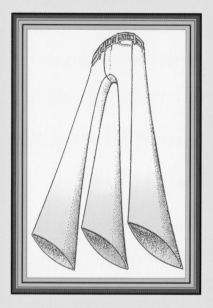

Can you see what's wrong with
this pair of bell-bottoms?

Observe this cow very carefully.
Do you notice anything unusual
about it?

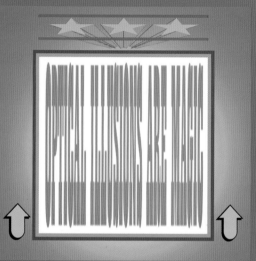

Can you read this secret message?
Tilt the page to eye level and look
in the direction of the arrows with
one eye closed.

A farmer put up this sign. Can you understand what he was trying to say?

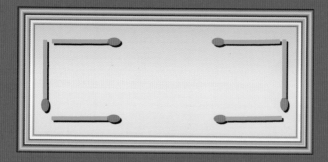

In just one move, can you
make the matches form
a complete oblong shape?

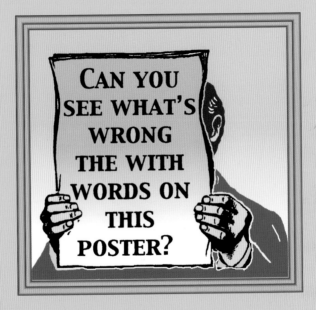

Can you see what's wrong
with this poster?

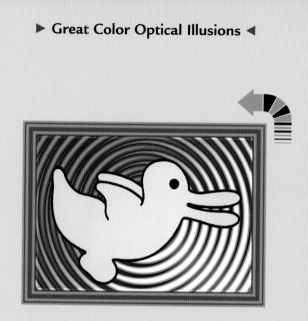

How do you turn a duck
into a rabbit?

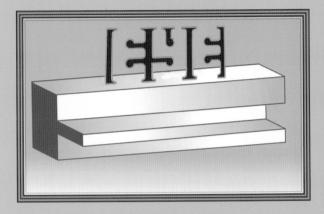

Can you figure out the meaning of the shapes on the top shelf? And what's unusual about the structure?

Is the star closer to the top or
the base of the mountain?

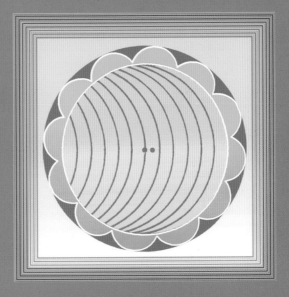

Which of these two dots
is in the true center?

Without turning the page upside down, describe this man. Is he happy or sad? Now check to find out.

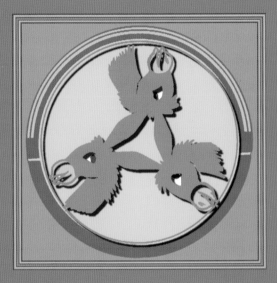

What is strange about
these donkeys?

What's wrong with this picture?

We hope that you have enjoyed the optical illusions in this book. Now, a final thought. To find out what happens to all good things, just turn this page upside down.

Page

4   It says, "We see but **we we** don't observe."

5   The zebra is descended from a solid black animal. The white stripes are superficial tufts on the black background color of the animal's skin.

6   The old lady's face shows her life. You can see her as a baby, a young girl, courting, in marriage, and finally in death. This type of art is based on the work of Archimboldo, a painter who lived in Italy from 1517 to 1593.

7   Turn the page upside down to see them smiling. Now they are married.

8   The young woman's chin becomes the nose of the old lady.

9   It looks like an old Asian man. Daniel Webster's shirt forms his forehead.

10   The drum appears to spin. The word "rotator" is a palindrome; it reads the same backwards and forwards.

11   Mona Lisa.

12   Look closely and you'll find the profiles of Adam and Eve. The phrase "Madam I'm Adam"

is a palindrome; it reads the same backwards and forwards.

13   Turn the page 90° counterclockwise. His face will appear.

14   The circle appears to be in two different shades of color.

15   Bring the page close to your face. The bee and flower will come together.

16   Pile B. Were you surprised? Measure each of them to check.

17   A black cat down a coal mine eating a stick of licorice at midnight.

18   The secret word is "hello." Look at the page in the direction of the arrow at eye level.

19   It changes direction!

20   Look at the reflection of this page in the mirror.

21   At first glance, you see a bearded man. On closer inspection, you'll find a phoenix.

22   Turn the page upside down and you will see the mother's head. The baby's diaper becomes the mother's head scarf.

23   It appears to follow you, but it's just an illusion. This design was used as a recruiting poster for the British Army.

24   Turn the page upside down and you will see a slice of cake. The name "Otto" has both horizontal and vertical symmetry. And it's also a palindrome!

25   The choice is yours!

26   Bring the page closer to your face. The figures will come together.

27   Take your pick!

28   No. The set of stairs is impossible.

29   They are both the same size. Trace one of them and measure it against the other. Their curve tricks us and creates the illusion.

30   It depends on what direction you see the bird flying. Either answer is correct.

31   The letter E. Try looking at the page from a distance.

32   The right eye and bridge of the nose form the heads of Romeo and Juliet. This form of art was popular in the 19th century in Europe.

33   The choice is yours. It all depends on what you saw first. Horizontally, it reads A, B, C. Vertically, it reads 12, 13, 14.

34   A person riding a horse. See the illustration.

35   A part of Hearn's act is shown close-up. From a distance, it resembles the performer.

36   They are both the same height. The lines of perspective help to create the illusion of one being taller than the other.

37   You will see a lightbulb with a glowing yellow center. Yellow is the reverse color to blue. These opposite colors are known as complementary colors.

38   The choice is yours. Did you notice that the caption says, "How many **can can** you see?"

39   Turn the page 90° clockwise to reveal the circus.

40 The message, made up from the pale background shapes, says, "Can you find the words."

41 Turn the page upside down and he looks exactly the same.

42 It's a dog curled up on a rug. Turn the page so that the arrow points upwards to reveal the dog.

43 The fourth one down reads "something."

44 Your guess is as good as mine. It's impossible to tell.

45 From a distance, it's a skull. Close up, it's a man and woman sitting at a table.

46 Turn the page upside down for the answer. It says "Life."

47 Look at the left side of the picture and you will see the profile of the farmer's face.

48 Yes, it's impossible. Count the number of steps. You can count three, nine, or five steps.

49   See the illustration.

50   It all depends on how you look at it.

51   Turn the page 90° counterclockwise.

52   Turn the page upside down. Then look at the
      reflection in a mirror and you will see the
      correct price is only 20¢.

53   The Three of Hearts (tree of hearts).

54   Turn the page upside down.

55   The face can belong to either the man or the
      woman.

56   It is a magic square. Each horizontal, vertical,
      and diagonal line of four numbers adds up to
      264. It also works if you turn it upside down.

57   Each circle will seem to revolve on its axis. The inner cog wheel will appear to rotate in the opposite direction.

58   It is supposed to be the longest sentence that still reads the same when you turn it upside down.

59   Turn the page upside down.

60   Look at the lion's mane. You will see some of the old British colonies: Canada, India, Australia, New Zealand, and African colonies.

61   Napoleon's silhouette is found between the two trees on the right.

62   The previous one was 1881. The next one will occur in the year 6009.

63   It's a crate. Look at the illustration. It's easier to see it with the added lines.

64   It says, "I've got **a a** big head."

65   There are six F's in the sentence.

66   You might see a medal or two people having
      an argument.

67   "X" marks their spot. See illustration.

68   The middle leg is impossible.

69   Look at the markings on the cow's back. You
      will see a map of the United Kingdom.

70   It says, "Optical illusions are magic."

71   To tie mules to.

72   Slowly bring the page closer to your face. At a
      certain point, the matches will join up.

73   Look at the sequence of the words. It says, "the with." It should be "with the."

74   Turn the page 90° counterclockwise.

75   The shapes spell the word "eye." The shelf is an impossible object.

76   The star is midway between the point and the base. Use a ruler and you'll see.

77   The blue dot that is on the line is in the center.

78   Turn the page upside down and it says, "Lots o' eggs."

79   Study the picture carefully and you'll see his face. His hat is formed from the dog's ear.

80   At first glance, we think he's happy. But he's really sad. We are not used to seeing faces upside down. Since the mouth and eyes have been inverted, he seems very weird when we look at him.

81   The three donkeys have only three ears among them!

82   Turn on the light. It's an impossible candelabra. A number of the holders seem to be suspended in midair.

83   It says, "The end."